The Etiquette of Social Media

How to Connect and Respond to Others in the World of Social Media

LEONARD KIM

Written by Leonard Kim
Edited by KP Wee, author of *Fess Up, Jessup!* and *Tom Candiotti: A Life of Knuckleballs*

Kim, Leonard
The Etiquette of Social Media

ISBN: 1500918539
ISBN-13: 9781500918538

TESTIMONIALS ABOUT LEONARD KIM

"Leonard Kim has a real good style."
James Altucher: American Hedge Fund Manager, Entrepreneur, Bestselling Author.

"Leonard Kim is a good soul committed to helping people like you. He presents life and work advice in a way that busy readers really appreciate and understand."
Terrence Yang: Startup Investor, Mentor. Founder, Yang Ventures. USC, Harvard Law. Ex-Wall Street.

"Leonard Kim is an amazing human being. I thank him for validating our existence with his beautiful words. I'm grateful for him - real authentic."
Holly Ridings: Runway and Print Model

"Leonard Kim is a nice guy. He has had many failures in life but has managed to pick himself up and reestablish himself as a better and nicer person. Leonard is really funny, honest, straight forward and sincere."
Virali Modi: Model, Inspirational Speaker.

Leonard Kim writes in a voice that not only evokes empathy, but candidly opens up about experiences many people can identify with.
Janelle Alicia Monroy: Writer

DEDICATION

I dedicate this book to my grandfather, Robert L. Landis. He showed me how to live like a true man, by sharing love with everyone whom I encounter.

I also wanted to thank everyone who has helped me create this book.

James Altucher and Erin Paige Law for inspiring me to follow my dream.

Marc Bodnick, Jay Wacker and Adam D'Angelo for providing a platform to write on.

Terrence Yang and Vivy Chao for helping me come up with the title.

Joshua M. Shelton for being an amazing friend and taking my photo.

Catheryn Chen for hiring me to be her consultant and for creating my cover.

KP Wee, Bhavesh Aggarwal, Melissa Stroud and Peter Flom for the thorough editing.

And you, the reader, for supporting me in this journey of translating knowledge into wisdom.

TABLE OF CONTENTS

	ACKNOWLEDGEMENTS	1
	PREFACE	3
1	INTRODUCTION	5
2	WHY ETIQUETTE IS IMPORTANT	9
3	VISIBILITY: CAN EVERYONE POTENTIALLY SEE WHAT I WRITE?	13
4	BE. DO. HAVE.	25
5	PERSONAL ETIQUETTE	33
6	RESEARCH AND WHY IT'S IMPORTANT	39
7	HOW TO INITIATE A CONVERSATION WITH A POTENTIAL FRIEND	43
8	HOW TO INITIATE A CONVERSATION WITH A POTENTIAL BUSINESS ASSOCIATE OR CLIENT	47
9	HOW TO SEEK OUT A MENTOR OR ASK FOR ADVICE	55
10	NASTY PEOPLE. TOXICITY AND ITS DOWNSIDES	59
11	THE IMPORTANCE OF SELF-CONTROL AND ZEN STUFF	63

12 HOW TO RESPOND TO NASTY COMMENTS   65

13 TIPS TO A HAPPY LIFESTYLE, LIKE DRINKING   69
    TEA AND HAPPY RELATIONSHIPS

14 CONCLUSION: START CONNECTING TODAY   73

15 BONUS CHAPTER: DON'T BE AWKWARD   75

ACKNOWLEDGMENTS

I wanted to thank Bianca Diesel, Jennie Kwon, Ellen Vrana, CamMi Pham, Grace Lee, Jessica Stafford, Kris Rosvold, David Mack, Clarrie Johnson, Evan Duning, Garrick Saito, Jason Chen, Allie Burke, Jagir Jhaveri, Thomas Chong, Allen Han, Rachel Laine, Shobhit Khinvasara, Holly Ridings, Bridgette Samonte, Helen He, Havi Pham, Rick Bruno, Susanna Mendler, Richard J. Kim, Kony Kim, Ian Thompson, Annie Dai, James Bae, Tom Byron, Shirley Xia, Valerie Cooper, Qiwen Liu, Dave Cheng, Deinis Matos, Sugy Yi, Xu Beixi, Joyce Kim, Elizabeth Leclair, Barbara Buckley, Elynn Lee, Kyle Murao, Janelle Monroy, Heidi Kabage, Jay Bazzinotti, Caroline Zelonka, Lyuda Morhun-Le, Dan Strayer, Kai Peter Chang, Carlo Silva, Minh Tran, Jane Chin, Giordon Stark, Hannah L. Cho, Amanda Tendler, Dave Braun, Clif Braun, Noam Kaiser, Mike Leary, Becky Lee, Graeme Shimmin, Trynh Nguyen, Jennifer Apacible, Ben Milnes, Katherine Fang, Skyler Oswald, Prachi Gupta, Darrell Harville, Mark Hamric, Anita Sanz, Cherie Nixon, Paul Denlinger, Varsha Iyer, Daniel Kim, Neha Sinha, Phil Chung, Abbe Diaz, Jeff Nelson, Stan Hanks, Hunter McCord, Agratha Dinakaran, Kiran Farooque, Virali Modi, Scott Danzig, Neil Patel, Viola Yee, Victor Liew Jia Hao, Larry Mancinelli, Danita Crouse, Alejandro Cardini May, James Liu, Cyndi Fink, Ariel Williams, Erica Friedman, Ahmed Khanzada, Cathy Lee, Dan Knight, Steve Black, Scott Balster, Fabiola Torres, Brett Miketta, Nicholas Smith, Martijn Sjoorda, Josh Lucas, Jeff Meyerson, Ridwa Mousa, Denis Oakley, Angus Tang, Gayle Laakman McDowell, Rory Young, Leonid Knyshov, Jay Mehta, Jesse Lashley, Christi Wentz, Desmond Hardy, Denise Tapp, David Min, Andrew Medal, Bryan Harris, Brady Chiu, Wing Chau, Dejoy Shastikk, Elyse Yang, Matt Wasserman, Robert J. Choi, Jamie Howard, Charles Faraone, Randy Vollrath, Josh Manson, Jaspal Singh, Jann Griffith Hoke, and Jane Dinh for inspiring me to continue to write.

PREFACE

It was another day in summer. I had just created a brand that was picking up momentum. A brand in myself. I was a year into my project. I had millions upon millions of views on my content. I was at a point in my brand where I needed to make a decision on what to do next.

I have a background as an executive at a few startups where I made something from nothing. So I thought, *'What should I do?'* Should I consult? Run an SaaS (Software as a Service) company? Create a personal development program? Look for a new executive level job?

Unsure of exactly what to do, I decided to take a break and quit everything for a while. In doing so, something surprising happened. I ended up finding a girlfriend. We shared our first moment together with ice cream. After she came to know me better and realized that I didn't really have any goals in life, she told me that I was like a kid in an adult's body. But I was on vacation from my responsibilities. So I figured it was time to get back into focus and start working again.

During my hiatus, I reached out to my mentor, best-selling author James Altucher. He was in Thailand, taking a break from life just before the release of his newest best-selling book, *The Power of No*. I sincerely asked him for advice. He told me that I should write short books. The idea made sense to me. It was something that I could do. I decided to share what I have learned over the years in the form of books.

I crowdsourced ideas on what to write about. After gathering a few ideas, I started to rank them according to importance. Then my friends Terrence Yang and Vivy Chao of Yang Ventures invited me out to dinner. Vivy Chao has an extensive background in education. She's been a professor, vice principal of a school, and currently works as a fellow at the Los Angeles Unified School District through Education Pioneers. She is also a blogger for *The Huffington Post*.

We were discussing the types of messages and comments that we receive on the Internet and how absurd they are. How some people send us their life stories, while others use cookie cutter platforms and don't even attempt to connect.

Having a background in education, Vivy mentioned how it is such a shame that with how new social media is our education system doesn't teach the etiquette of social media. Then it dawned upon me. With my experience on social media over the last few decades of my life, I had the know-how to provide my insights on the topic.

Thus came the inception of the idea of the book, *The Etiquette of Social Media*.

1 INTRODUCTION

Social media is paving the way of the future. It is everywhere, from Facebook to Twitter to Quora and LinkedIn. It's something fresh and new. So new, that how to behave with proper etiquette on the Internet has never been taught in our traditional schooling environment.

Without the proper guidelines to the etiquette of social media, some questions may have crossed your mind before picking up this book:

Should we act however we want online?

Should we censor ourselves?

Are we supposed to act civilized on certain platforms but casual on others?

How are we supposed to come across as civilized human beings on the Internet?

What happens if we encounter a bully?

Do we defend ourselves or do we fight back?

How do we strike up a conversation with a stranger?

How do we strike up a conversation with someone whom we have a romantic interest in?

How do we start a conversation with a potential business partner, client or future employer?

These are just a few of the questions that came across my mind before writing this book. To share what my experience has been on various social media platforms: From when I first joined AOL at the age of 16 back in 2001, to Xanga, Findapix, Myspace, LinkedIn, Twitter, Facebook, Quora, and the other platforms I have encountered along the way.

Some companies out there understand the importance of etiquette. Quora, an online knowledge market is one of them. Quora implements a rule on their site called BNBR, which stands for Be Nice, Be Respectful. The foundation on Quora's website is that they want to create a happy environment; an environment where everyone can feel comfortable writing and participating in discussions. In other words, they have a foundation to build upon.

Online colleges and universities are now adopting a similar philosophy on their discussion forums. They have had cases where their online forums went out of control. The reasons behind the colleges doing this was so that students with opposing views wouldn't attack each other. This seemed to have been a problem, where etiquette was not discussed before when new students joined a class. They would treat the online classes much like how they would their personal social media sites. This is becoming an ongoing trend. A trend that colleges needed to stop. Most colleges have now issued a standard set of guidelines for students to follow when posting on their internal forums on the Internet.

Other online websites like LinkedIn, Facebook, Twitter, etc. don't have any foundations or guidelines. You can say whatever you want and as long as isn't a link to porn or spam, your opinion stays documented. You can even use profanity. Nothing gets censored.

We all want to speak our mind when we're on the Internet. Sometimes we feel hurt and want to express ourselves. Other times we feel betrayed because a friend ditched us on the way to the movies and left us behind. Maybe we want to lash out for no reason because someone stole our money. Maybe all we want to do is talk about Becky's butt.

Or maybe something we read online will shock us. Other things upset us. Some content is so engaging that it makes us react. It frustrates us so much that you want to comment and give this person a piece of your mind.

The purpose of this book is to make you more aware of your surroundings. The Internet is bigger than any one of us can ever imagine. It is definitely a global platform where anyone and everyone lives. If our parents brought us up in an environment where etiquette matters, we know our elbows shouldn't be on the table when dining. This book should be utilized as a guide. A guide to help us understand how we should be acting online, especially when you are on center stage, in the public spotlight.

In each chapter, we will discuss key points and examples to each topic at hand. There may even be some practice exercises for you to try.

Join me on this journey as we discuss the etiquette of social media, and let's learn how beneficial it will be to your life as a whole.

2 WHY ETIQUETTE IS IMPORTANT

We all heard it before, whether it be from our mothers or from our significant others. When we go out to a fancy outing, such as a wedding or an exquisite cocktail party, we have to be on our P's and Q's. In other words, to be on our best behavior.

During these events, we have to do many things so we don't embarrass ourselves, or the people whom we are with. Or we end up looking like slobs. We can't put our shoulders on the table. We have to use the chilled fork for salad. We have to speak in the proper tone, without any slang. The list goes on and on.

Why do we bother with keeping up such appearances at these types of events?

It's just a long tradition. It's the way we were meant to interact in such settings. But it gets even deeper than that.

People judge each other. We will think of a person as clean, neat, uncouth, sloppy, well spoken, a loose cannon, and so forth. I know, I know. You've heard that you shouldn't judge a book by its cover. However, we all do it, whether we want to admit it or not. It's just human nature.

Should we care about what other people think about us?

Yes and no.

The answer is a little more complex than it seems. It really depends. There are a lot of factors that come into play, such as who is in the environment, what impact they have on our lives, and if what we do will either embarrass us or open up doors to new friendships and opportunities.

Much like how these events determine how we act in a public setting, the Internet is another place where etiquette is important. Sometimes, it may be difficult to understand this, because you may be using the Internet at your home in your pajamas. People can't see what you're wearing in the comfort of your own home, but they can still see what you write on the Internet.

Whether you are 18 or 88, in school or entering into retirement, we aren't going to be exactly where we are today for the rest of our lives. What we say speaks volume, of who we are. We need to tread lightly and think before we speak, because behind every corner, there is an unknown stranger who is building a case either for or against us.

In the Internet age, each individual person is their own independent brand. If you are unsure of what a brand is, think Nike, Coca-Cola or even Apple. When we think of these words, certain images come to our mind.

Nike, for example portrays an image of athletic mavens who are at the forefront of their careers. Professional players in national sports ranging from basketball to track and field to rugby and soccer. Even Olympian athletes resemble the Nike brand.

Coca-Cola, on the other hand, portrays an image of a refreshing beverage. A beverage that you can share with a friend or significant other. One that even spreads happiness to other creatures, polar bears especially.

Apple portrays the image of pure innovation. They understand the concept of supply and demand and how to make the market want what they create. Whether it be the new MacBook or iPhone, people line up in front of stores for hours just to get their hands on the newest devices.

Considering these three brands and the images that they portray, we have to think about who we are as our own independent brand. Do we want to portray ourselves to the world as someone who is ill mannered, unkempt, or even uneducated? Or do we want to portray ourselves as lovable smart people who are in high demand?

Now, this doesn't mean to be a fake person. Absolutely not. It's more along the lines of being aware of what you are saying. To think before you speak. Or in this case, since we are on the Internet, to think before you write.

It can almost be seen as censorship, but I see it more as polishing our behavior around others. Much like how you wouldn't want to be seen as a fool in the middle of a black tie event for wearing a yellow blouse or tie, you don't want to be seen as a fool on the Internet either.

So why is etiquette important?

It's to save face when you potentially have millions of eyeballs on everything that you do.

3 VISIBILITY: CAN EVERYONE POTENTIALLY SEE WHAT I WRITE?

Throughout the Internet, there are hundreds of millions of sites. Some that we consider to be private, while many, many others that the entire world can see. Sometimes, these sites may cross over and we may not even be aware that this is happening.

Our words have a lasting impact. People will judge us for everything we say. Sometimes, we have to wonder if what we say is safe from the views of outside spectators. Other times, we assume that it is. I want to discuss what impact our word has and touch upon privacy settings. Of course, the safest route would be to carry etiquette through all social media outlets. However, sometimes we just want moments where we can just express exactly what is on our mind.

To start off, we will be discussing the most popular social network on the Internet: Facebook. Then we will get into other platforms, such as: LinkedIn, YouTube, Twitter, Instagram, Quora, Reddit, and posts written on forums or news sites.

Facebook is one of the trickiest online media outlets on the Internet. It takes a sense of awareness to figure out whether others can see what we write or not. Sometimes, we may feel extremely safe with the platform. That might cause us to unintentionally say something private in a public environment. It can be tough to filter each thing we say to come out as a proper speaking individual. However, the consequences of not doing so can be detrimental.

Imagine if you wrote something two years ago that expressed your extreme distaste. Or something you had posted when intoxicated. What if a potential employer saw it? Do you think that could impact whether they hire you? How about a potential significant other? A friend who has opposing views? The admissions board to a college? Or even a classmate or coworker who you have to do a project with.

Recently, I interviewed my good friend, Grace Lee. She is the Director of Marketing at *JobKoreaUSA.com*, a Radio Korea company. She also acts as the Director of Special Events at APEX | Asian Professional Exchange, a 501(c)3 which acts as a medium to bring increased awareness about and to Asian Americans through community service, fellowship, charitable fundraisers, cultural events, professional networking and educational seminars.

I asked Grace Lee this specific question, "Have you ever encountered a situation where you saw that a credible applicant was overlooked for a job due to something they had written or done on social media?"

Grace Lee responded, "We encountered a credible applicant whom we felt would be an ideal fit at our company. Later, we examined this candidate's social media profiles. He had disturbing photos of himself. He literally had photos of trash and half eaten foods on his profile page. It was really gross. There weren't even any comments on the posts. He gave off the impression that he does not have an organized life. Afterwards, we considered him unfit to handle the professional role that he would have to partake in with our company."

In life, we encounter many situations where we are brought out of our comfort zone. Sometimes, we are to meet with other individuals we know nothing about. Social media profiles have changed the way we behave both on the Internet and in person. It has almost become second nature to Google the person we are meeting, or for the person we are meeting to Google us. Next to everything that we say on the Internet could be displayed in these search results.

In 2013, Kaplan Test Prep did their annual study on College Admissions Officers. They came to find that 29% (up from 27%) of these Admissions Officers Googled an applicant, 31% (up from 26%) had visited their Facebook page to learn more about the candidates and 30% (down from 35%) found something online about an applicant that negatively impacted their college application. [1]

How embarrassing would it be if what you thought to be your private thoughts were shared on Google? What if they were the reason that prevented you from getting into the college of your dreams, landing a new job, a business partnership or even a relationship with a significant other?

What if it was because you were unfamiliar with these privacy settings?

How do we avoid these mistakes?

Having a full understanding of privacy settings is essential, along with the impact of our visibility.

As most people do, when we are on Facebook, we make assumptions. We assume that since Facebook is a network of friends and family, that what we say is private. What makes it harder is that we can update these social networks straight from our phone, making it even more difficult to judge.

[1] https://www.kaptest.com/assets/pdfs/College_Admissions_Officers_Survey_2013.pdf

Before we update a post, in the bottom right corner, we have access to our privacy settings.

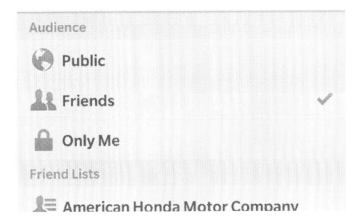

We can choose who we want to see our posts.

- Public

- Friends

- Only me

Sometimes, we may forget what setting we choose. It is important to always check which privacy setting we are choosing before each post.

Want to share a picture of your cat doing a trick? It may be in your best interest to keep that a private post just between your friends. How about when you are out partying with friends? That should be private as well. Celebrating a promotion? That could be a public post.

It takes some time to figure out and filter which posts should be public and which should be private. After some practice, you will get better at this.

Where the problem lies is not in posting content on your own page. It is when posting or commenting on the pages of friends or public pages.

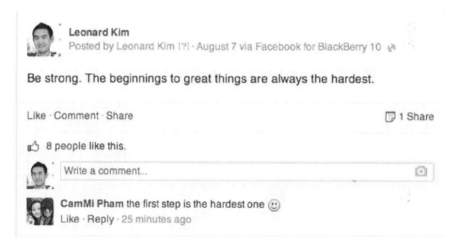

Everything written on a public page is public. Look how CamMi comments on my public page.

World Facts
July 1

Beyoncé is now the worlds most powerful celebrity, according to Forbes.

Like · Comment · Share   👍173 💬10 🔗2 Shares

👍 173 people like this.   Top Comments ▾

Write a comment...

Demetrius Aaron Who gives a ~~fuck~~
Like · Reply · 👍7 · July 1 at 7:33am

Tumo C. Mukani It ain't that much of a shocker.
Like · Reply · 👍6 · July 1 at 7:02am

Falenderimi Takon Allahut No one gives a ~~shit~~
Like · Reply · 👍2 · July 1 at 8:06am

Tara Flynn She's a piece of garbage
Like · Reply · 👍1 · July 3 at 9:42am

Audie Marie Shay Janina Barry
Like · Reply · 👍1 · July 1 at 6:59pm

Junior Mfgee Shes still ratchet lol
Like · Reply · 👍1 · July 1 at 12:36pm

Oliver Gwop because she got the power to sick her little sister on your ~~ass~~
Like · Reply · 👍1 · July 1 at 7:32am

Now look at this other public page. I have never met any of these people. However, I can see everything they wrote on this page.

We all have to be quite cautious when posting anything onto a public page, or they can even be circulated into a book like this one.

Imagine you were an employer. After reading what Demetrius Aaron, Falendrerimi Takon Allahut, Tara Flynn, Junior Mfgee or Oliver Gwop said, would you still consider hiring them?

I know I wouldn't. So be cautious of what you write on public pages, because it will follow you around.

We also have to be extra careful when we write on a friend's page.

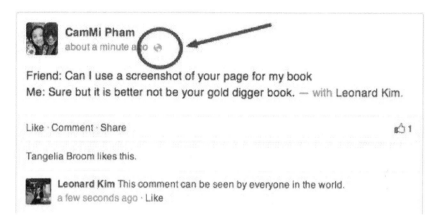

This is a status update that my friend CamMi Pham wrote. See that picture of the globe on the image above?

That means that everything that is posted on this particular status update can be seen by everyone. We need to be extra careful when commenting on a post of this nature.

This is another status update by CamMi Pham. See how there are two people? That means that the conversation can be seen by both either her friends or my friends.

But yet, this is where things can get tricky. What if CamMi were to go back to her older posts and make them public?

Your post would be visible to anyone and everyone as well.

Is it likely that this would happen?

No.

But it could happen. Sometimes, if someone says something cruel to me on one of my posts that circulates to my friends, I change my privacy setting to public.

Is it nice?

No. But if they feel they want to say something unkind to me, then I'm going to let them eat their words.

The best thing to do would be to play it safe and share content that has a sense of etiquette to it on all the pages of Facebook.

Websites like LinkedIn allow comments on their posts as well. If you are unfamiliar with LinkedIn, it is a social platform for business professionals. People network on the site for jobs and other hiring opportunities. Being a professional network, we would assume that most people will try to bring a sense of etiquette with them onto this platform. It seems that this isn't the case though.

I publish articles on LinkedIn. Sometimes, I get positive comments. Other times, I get comments that rip straight into me. Remember, LinkedIn is filled with recruiters and top level executives scouting out talent.

I posted an article titled: *This founder's ego got in his way of making decisions. You wouldn't believe what happened next.* It had attained 3,772 views. This is an example of two comments I received.

Close to 3,000 people saw what they wrote. Now, everyone who is reading this book will see it too.

We can all agree that LinkedIn is a social network for professionals. With that in mind, what do you think of their behavior? Would you give them a pass, since there was never a guide for the etiquette of social media? Or would you hold them to the public words they said?

Would you want to do business with any of these people who wrote these comments? How about the companies that they work for? As a hiring manager, would you bring either of them to represent your company?

These are important questions you need to ask yourself before you write anything on the Internet. But yet, more so on a platform like LinkedIn.

YouTube is a little more tricky, since there are so many comments on each video that is posted. Everything we post is seen by everyone though. So use your discretion when typing up that comment of how amazing you thought Britney Spears was when TMZ snapped that picture of her going into that one club.

With Twitter and Instagram, nearly everything is public. A few people have private Twitter and Instagram accounts, but they are few and far in between. Most people post content that can be seen by everyone. Then there are even posts that mention people or have hashtags.

What is a hashtag?

A hashtag is a word or phrase preceded by a hash or pound sign (#) and used to identify messages on a specific topic.

Posts of this nature are broadcast to an even wider audience than who follows you or the users your comments go on. Use extreme discretion when commenting on something with a hashtag.

What does it mean when someone mentions someone?

It means that everyone who follows who you mention can see the posts as well.

Here is an example of both the hash tag and the @ symbol being used.

Elizabeth Dehn @ElizabethDehn · Aug 7
Hi @MrLeonardKim,
Thank you for this article! #Inspiring and #simple lnkd.in/bsbGPmY

LinkedIn

How To Serve Humanity and Where You Can Start
By Leonard Kim @MrLeonardKim

On Quora and Reddit, people can pose questions, which have answers. Quora requires users to abide to a real name policy, while Reddit allows users to hide behind a screen name. People may think that these sites are closed networks where they can say anything they want, but questionable activity may end up getting you banned from these platforms. Leaving comments under your real name is something else to worry about entirely, since it can all end up in search engines.

You want to stay away from saying something like this. It could have a huge negative impact on your life. An example of that would be Brendan Eich. He was forced to resign from Firefox due to his social beliefs.

Quora and Reddit posts are also sometimes reshaped into articles on regular media outlets, such as Fortune, Forbes, Huffington Post, and many other sites. These sites all link back to these posts, which could cause even more dismay.

Writing comments on sites like these can be even more harmful, because millions of people read the news. When a million eyeballs are on your comment, those few words could end up defining who you are.

Now it's important to understand that these principles don't only apply to what you write. It also applies to the pictures you post and other content you like. Did you enjoy a provocative video of a group of girls doing stretches from behind? Or an article that emphasized controversial viewpoints about hatred? No matter what social media site you're on, clicking "like," "favorite," or "upvote" on that image or article would cause it to spread into the news feed of everyone who follows you, with your name attached to it. The lesson here: Avoid liking controversial content that could jeopardize your image.

When taking part in social media, the first step is to understand visibility. We all have to understand that our words have consequences. So make sure to think twice before posting that rude comment, or it may end up eternalized in a book.

4 BE. DO. HAVE.

This chapter may seem a little off topic to the main purpose of this book, etiquette. However, understanding this concept is quite important in all aspects of your life.

Take a moment to participate in an exercise. Get out a piece of paper. Write down everything you want in your life.

Whether it be a BMX bike or a six pack, write it down. It can even be a desired life partner or a successful career. Just write everything down.

This is an exercise to get your brain muscles working, so you can understand what is truly important to you. After you gather together this list, rank them by importance.

What is at the top of the list?

Think hard about that.

Why is it ranked at the top of the list?

At first, it may be hard to identify. Maybe you won't even understand why you put it there in the first place. So this brings us to our second step.

Ask yourself why. Then answer. Ask yourself why again. Then answer. Then do it again, until you have done it five times.

To show you how this works, I interviewed CamMi Pham, Digital Strategist of KwinMedia. This is how our conversation went:

What do you want most in life?

I want knowledge.

Why do you want knowledge?

Knowledge is a powerful tool.

Why is knowledge a powerful tool?

If I want material things, they will last until I exhaust my resources.

If I want money, it will move from my pocket to someone else's.

If I want power, one day someone will steal it from me.

If I want fame, it will fade away.

With knowledge, no matter what happens in my life, it will remain with me. With the right knowledge, I can change the world and get everything else I mentioned.

People spend their entire life to learn these lessons. In the digital age, we are lucky to be able to easily access to all the knowledge we want with little to no cost. With the right knowledge, we will have the power to leverage other people's strength to create an even bigger impact.

Why do you want to create a big impact?

The best part in life is the journey, not the destination. Wealth, power and fame are relative. We will always compare ourselves to someone who has more than we do. It will never be enough.

Investing in people will give us the highest return.

Why do you feel that investing in people will give us the highest return?

It was the way my family was raised. It lasts for generations. Our success will reflect in other people's lives.

Big power, wealth and fame come with big responsibilities. Everything we do will have an impact on others. I don't want to create a big impact because I want to be the next Gandhi. I am not that ambitious. Instead, I want to invest kindness into people. I hope one day the people whom I invest kindness into will help my family when they need it.

Why do you want people to help your family when they need it?

Because life is a roller coaster. We can make predictions about what is going to happen but nobody can know exactly how the future is going to turn out. If you are wealthy or powerful, you can buy information to make it easier to predict. But at the end of the day, you still can't say you control the future. There are a million unpredictable things happening around the world. Any of them can change your life.

I was born in old money, grew up with the new money, and have no money. When my family lost everything we had, nobody was there. I realized how lonely fame, wealth and power made us. When I had money, my friends knew who we were. When I had no money, I knew who my friends were. All I had left was my family. Don't get me wrong, I don't blame other people. Everyone has their own life, and they need to take care of themselves first. My family is the people who will always stand next me through all the good and bad days.

The dream of the red chamber is one of the 4 classics of ancient China. The story is about the rise and fall of the two most powerful aristocratic families in the capital of China. When I was small, my mother always told me the story of Granny Liu, elderly country rustic and a distant relative of a Lady Wang. Wang Xifeng was the only person from the 2 families who treats Granny Liu with a kind heart. When the families ended up disfavored by the Emperor, then all the wealth, power and fame faded away. Granny visited Wang Xifeng before she died and saved her daughter from entering concubinage, or prostitution. She took the young girl home and raised her. My mother reminded me to be kind to everyone, one day I need someone to treat my family and me the same way.

From CamMi's interview, we can see how this process triggers a specific thought process. She put knowledge at the top of her list of desires. When asked why she wants knowledge, we can see that she sees it as a tool. Each question gets deeper into the reasons why she feels that she should get all the knowledge possible. At the end, she remembers an event from her childhood. An event of her youth that has helped shape her into who she is today.

How this process works is simple. After we come up with each answer, we ask why based upon those answers. By doing this, we can reflect back to a specific moment that defined our lives. Much like how CamMi talks about how her family lost everything, you will find an event that reshaped your life as well. Then we can understand what we truly want in life and why we want it. They say that in life, when the why is strong enough, the how becomes easy.

I implore you to find out your *why*. Try this for yourself by utilizing the exercise on the next page.

EXERCISE:

1. What I want in life (ranked by order of importance):

[ ] _____   [ ] _____

[ ] _____   [ ] _____

[ ] _____   [ ] _____

[ ] _____   [ ] _____

[ ] _____   [ ] _____

2. Go back and rank each item by importance.

3. Ask yourself why you want this. Then answer. Next, ask yourself why, based off of your answers. Do this five times.

Why? _____

_____

Why? _____

_____

Why? _____

_____

Why? _____

_____

Why? _____

_____

Why is this exercise important and what does it have to do with etiquette?

Great question.

The exercise is important because when we are able to identify our desires, we can understand what our purpose is in life. My friend Thomas has always asked me to introduce him to women. At first, I thought he just wanted company of people of the opposite sex. Then one time, I did this exercise with him. The reasoning behind why he wanted me to introduce him to women was so pure. He didn't even know how pure it was, until he went through the process himself.

At the end of the exercise, we will come to a conclusion. We will figure out what we want to have in our life. Then we will need to face some misconceptions.

As people, we are all under the impression that in order to have what we want, we must do what it takes to get it. Most people are missing the most essential step though. Before we do what it takes, we must first become the person who deserves to have what we want.

Remember that exercise we did when we figured out what we really wanted in life? This is where it comes in handy. That list and the reasons behind why you chose what you did will be your fuel. That will help you do what it takes to have what you desire. But before that, you must first become the person who deserves these types of things.

What type of people deserve these things?

People who carry etiquette in all aspects of their life, especially on social media.

So how does this chapter relate to etiquette?

It is to relate the importance of why you should carry etiquette in all aspects of your life, especially on social media.

Let's say that in the exercise, you said that you wanted to be wildly successful, financially. All of us believe that what we need to do is go out there, put our head down and work. If we work hard enough, we will become wildly successful. But now, let's take a step back. Think of all the successful people that you see in magazines.

Forbes Billionaires: Full List Of The World's 500 Richest People is a great example. Think about how these people act. Do they carry themselves with their shoulders slouched? Do they wear whatever they want? Do they skip out on showers? Do they eat with their shoulders on the table?

Now think about how they act when they're on the Internet.

Do these people use slang when they write? Do they defame others? Do they attack people? Do they write rude comments? Or type lyk diz?

No, they don't. These people come across as idea citizens who have mastered the art of etiquette, both online and in the real world. Because they have mastered these skills of etiquette, along with carrying the mentality of a successful person, they were able to have what they wanted most in life.

By carrying out **The Etiquette of Social Media,** you too can follow the first step of becoming who you need to be to have what you desire. Or, at least come across as a proper and likable human being on the Internet. Either way, you win.

So let's continue onward on how you can master the etiquette of social media.

5 PERSONAL ETIQUETTE

Here we are. In the most important chapter of them all. The chapter where we outline the be in the equation of be, do, have. Personal etiquette.

Personal etiquette can be seen as how you tie a tie when you go out to a red carpet event. Or how you place a napkin on your lap when it is time to eat. Online, there are many things that we can do to make sure we come across as civil human beings.

The first thing we want to do is use grammar properly. We see grammar nazis everywhere. To be caught by one of them can be quite embarrassing. When we mean to say you're, sometimes we say your. It can be hard to distinguish what goes where. I would recommend carrying around a dictionary to understand this better. However, if you are still unsure of what goes where, I would suggest that you run it by a friend before posting. What the French call a faux pas, which is one of the worst things we can do, is write with improper grammar on the Internet. It can be quite embarrassing as well.

Another mistake that many people do online is when dey typ lik diz. They use text speak on the Internet, as if people can understand what they are writing. Quite honestly, I don't even know what I wrote, so I'm certain that others wouldn't understand it as well.

We don't even need to be experts at grammar and spelling. All we need to do is be aware when the red squiggly line comes about and use your and you're in the right places. Personally, I like writing at a fifth grade level so everyone can understand what I write. It makes it easier for people to relate to the message I communicate.

I even flipped through a few pages of a Game of Thrones book by George R. R. Martin. He writes at a fifth-grade level. His writing was good enough to be turned into a TV series. So communicating at a fifth grade level is optimal when carrying etiquette on social media platforms.

The next step is to think before you speak. There are a lot of articles on the Internet. Some will rile us up. Others will be stupid. If you decide to comment on these articles, remember a few things. There is an author, a real human who wrote these articles on the other end of the site. Attacking the author can hurt their feelings, especially if you talk about how poorly their work is written. If you are opposing their views, everyone can see what you write. Tread lightly and make sure to not offend anyone.

One thing I do is wait around 30 minutes before stating my opinion, so I can gather my thoughts and clean out any attacks within my response. I do my best to first compliment the author about their viewpoints, state what I agree with, then touch upon what I disagree with as to enter a civilized discussion. You don't want to get into heated debates on the Internet. This gets publicized for the world to see.

Another thing that you can do is follow Quora's policy of BNBR, or Be Nice Be Respectful. Quora goes into full detail of the policy on their site:

The Be Nice, Be Respectful policy is a Quora policy and core principle that requires that users treat other users on the site with civility and respect.

Overview

A core Quora principle ("*Be Nice, Be Respectful*") requires that people treat other people on the site with civility, respect, and consideration. Assume that others on the site are also trying to make it a great resource. Respect opposing or differing opinions, beliefs and conclusions. Try to listen to and understand others you may disagree with. Encourage others on the site to also be welcoming and respectful.

Attacking people or content

Personal attacks are not allowed on Quora, nor are disrespectful or insulting attacks directed at other people's content. People should be civil and respectful in disagreement with others and should not (1) make attacks or otherwise disparage other people, (2) refer to other people's content with insulting or disrespectful language, or (3) harass others on the site. These behaviors hurt the Quora community and deter users from helping to create a better resource.

Do your best to see the world from the perspective of the person who posted the question (the original poster ["OP"]) or answer. It is often not helpful to criticize or challenge the fundamental beliefs of the OP (in an answer) or answerer (in a comment). For example, in responding to the question "Is it OK to only go to church on Easter?", the following answer would be considered disrespectful and is not allowed: "There is no God and religious rituals are a waste of time." Use good judgement and be empathetic. Answers and comments that challenge the fundamental beliefs of an OP or answerer will be held to a very high standard re: Be Nice, Be Respectful.

Comment threads & how to disagree in comments

In general, comment threads on Quora are interactions among strangers. Given that another person on the site may be new to Quora and/or doesn't know you, we require a higher level of politeness than other interactive platforms where users know one another and/or where more adversarial social norms are established and tolerated. A key goal of the Be Nice, Be Respectful policy is ensure that comments do **not** discourage or intimidate other people on Quora.

Disagreement and debate on Quora is encouraged and is often important to making the page more helpful. It is OK to disagree as long as your comments are civil, respectful, and polite, and as long as you give the impression of assuming good will on the part of the person you are disagreeing with. A good way of framing this test is: "If I am new to Quora and / or don't know you, would it be reasonable for me to perceive your comment as hostile or disrespectful toward me or what I've written?" The answer should be no.

In multi-comment threads where there is significant disagreement among people, a person should stop commenting on the thread before creating the reasonable impression that they are harassing, attacking, and/or bullying another person.

Examples

Examples of behaviors that violate the "Be Nice, Be Respectful" policy include:

- Personal attacks, including hurtful, insulting, or hostile comments.

- Making unjustified accusations against other user(s).

- Engaging in a pattern of behaviour that constitutes harassment of a targeted person or persons, e.g., by making threats, repeated annoying and unwanted contacts, repeated personal attacks, or posting personal information.

- Racial, sexual, homophobic, ageist, religious, political, ethnic, or other epithets directed against another contributor.

- Using someone's affiliations as a means of dismissing or discrediting their views (this does not include pointing out a conflict of interest of relevance to the discussion at hand).

- Speculating on the real life identity of an anonymous user.

Harassment

Harassment is defined as offensive behavior that appears to a reasonable observer to have the purpose of adversely affecting a targeted person or persons. The intended outcome may be to make using Quora unpleasant for the target, to undermine them, or to discourage them from editing and using the site. Examples of harassment include (but are not limited to): (1) making threats, (2) repeated annoying and unwanted contacts, (3) posting the personal information of another person, (4) using sexually explicit, profane, adversarial, or flirtatious language toward another person if such language would likely make the person uncomfortable.

Hate speech

Users are not allowed to post content or adopt a tone that would be interpreted by a reasonable observer as a form of hate speech, particularly toward a race, gender, religion, nationality, ethnicity, political group, sexual orientation or another similar characteristic. Questions and question details about generalizations in these topics should be phrased as neutrally and respectfully as possible.

Retaliation is not OK

It is never OK to violate the Be Nice, Be Respectful policy, even in response to another person who has violated the policy.

Please note that the Be Nice, Be Respectful policy also pertains to content posted by users who no longer use Quora.

Racial and ethnic slurs

Using any of the words on Wikipedia's list of ethnic slurs is not allowed in questions, answers, or comments, unless the purpose is to ask a sincere question about the usage/background of the word.

Messages

The Be Nice, Be Respectful policy applies to Messages on Quora.

Consequences

- Content that violates this policy may be reported to and removed by admins, and violations of this policy can result in a warning, comment blocking, an edit-block, or a ban.

- Depending on the severity of the Be Nice, Be Respectful violation, a user may be banned immediately (i.e., without waiting for content warnings or edit-blocks). People who appear to be using Quora for the primary purpose of harassing others may be banned without warning.

Block first before reporting violations

If you feel that another person is violating this policy with respect to you or your content, you should block them in addition to reporting them to moderation. [2]

Remember, the most important part of etiquette is to be fully aware of your surroundings. Think of how other people are viewing what you write. Your words are how the world sees you, so be calm and generous with what you say.

Which leads us to our next chapter...

[2] https://www.quora.com/Be-Nice-Be-Respectful-Quora-policy/What-is-Quoras-Be-Nice-Be-Respectful-policy

6 RESEARCH AND WHY IT'S IMPORTANT

Research.

In school, our teachers have taught us the importance behind this concept. When we write essays, we need to make sure that our points have documentation that states how we came to our conclusion. Even when solving math equations, our teachers ask us to show our work.

When working in a business environment, research is even more important than when in a classroom. In school, our teachers taught us to dot our i's and cross our t's. In other words, do our due diligence on matters even when they may seem to be of minor value. Sometimes, when dealing with a major business transaction, not looking into all the details can cause a deal to fall apart.

When we are on the Internet, we are going to want to do many things. We might want to comment on someone's status update, article, or video. We may even want to meet with new potential friends, lovers, business associates, clients, or mentors.

Imagine reading something online that was interesting. What if you were so compelled to respond to what you had read that you decided to comment before you did your research or even share the article with a friend?

On Facebook, I see this a lot. People share an article online that they presume to be true, but is in fact a myth. One article that comes to mind that people shared many times over the Internet was of a lawsuit between Apple and Samsung.

Back in August of 2012, Apple had sued Samsung and won 1.05 billion US dollars due to a patent infringement case. In the article that users shared all over the Internet, the message stated:

> Samsung Pays Apple $1 Billion Sending 30 Trucks Full of 5 Cents Coins
>
> This morning more than 30 trucks filled with 5-cent coins arrived at Apple's headquarters in California. Initially, the security company that protects the facility said the trucks were in the wrong place, but minutes later, Tim Cook (Apple CEO) received a call from Samsung CEO explaining that they will pay $1 billion dollars for the fine recently ruled against the South Korean company in this way.
>
> The funny part is that the signed document does not specify a single payment method, so Samsung is entitled to send the creators of the iPhone their billion dollars in the way they deem best. [3]

This particular article comes to mind because I even shared it myself, before fact checking. The problem with this myth was that a major news outlet had shared the article. Then a company by the name of *Snopes*, a myth busting media outlet, blew apart the article stating it was a complete myth.

[3] http://www.snopes.com/politics/satire/samsung.asp#8HijhEQ46JRQUT2j.99

We all ended up looking stupid for sharing a rumor that we presumed to be true.

If we were to take our time and fact check before sharing an article of this nature then we could save face. We come across as a more level headed person who doesn't buy into all the hype. We come across as someone who is reliable. More so, as someone who doesn't jump onto the bandwagon and spread hype just because everyone else does.

Imagine if we were in a different situation. A situation where you had commented on an article of this nature, stating how you thought it was hilarious. Let's say that article stayed for years, until this day. What if you were running a business and went to fundraise money from an angel investor? Or what if you were talking to a hiring manager for a position in due diligence or finance? What if they came across this article in a Google search and saw your comment on an article that *Snopes* proved to be false? Would that hinder your results to getting financing for your business or hired into the position you were looking to get?

What you say on the Internet stays up forever. To avoid mistakes that may affect us in the future, we need to be thorough.

Now research is even more than just saving face. There are times that you will want to meet specific people. Research is even more important in situations like these. I will go over a few situations in the next few chapters where research will give you a better chance at attaining your goals.

7 HOW TO INITIATE A CONVERSATION WITH A POTENTIAL FRIEND

As we have begun to move into the digital age, online friendships are becoming more common. We can meet people anywhere in the world, whether it be the United States, Europe, India or even Australia. All we need to do is turn on the computer, then go onto a social media platform, a forum, or a knowledge market, then exchange words.

We can connect to any person in the world. When we type a name in Google, we can find out about almost anyone in the world. With certain search filters we can even search country, state, or city.

When online, we may want to encounter new friends. The easiest way to make friends is to find people who have similar interests to you. Birds of a feather tend to flock together. So if you like certain things, then chances of you getting along with someone else who shares the same interests would be high.

Most people can think of their interests off the top of their head. They enjoy basketball, soccer, programming, or stocks. If you are aware of what you like, then it is easy to identify where on the Internet to hang out. All you have to do is search for communities that share your common interest.

Not all people have it that easy though. If you are like me, then you might not know what your interests are. That is why I joined Quora, which is a knowledge market. Since Quora has users of all demographics and interest groups, I had an endless supply of topics that I could choose to follow. Not knowing exactly what my interests are, I decided to follow as many topics as I could. Then I unfollowed the topics that did not interest me.

After I was able to sort the topics to only see what I wanted to see, I started to read the news feed. I saw some remarkable content and decided to follow some writers. If something resonated well with me, I commented on what they had written. I was doing my research by reading about these people whom I wanted to be friends with; by piecing together their lives.

Most people on the Internet share stories about themselves. They talk about their trials, tribulations, victories, interests, and passions. Some users even divulge personal information about their families. Our goal in connecting with others to make friends is to piece together a profile of who we want to meet.

Examples:

My friend Melissa Stroud is an active user on Quora. I live in Los Angeles. She lives in Arizona. We have shared interests that include fashion. She has shared a lot about her personal journey in life, including a situation where she was *this close* to homeless. It would be nice if we all came from middle-class families and never had a worry in the world. But we don't.

Melissa and I shared some things in common aside from just fashion. We both have had rough lives. By being able to read over her content and see how much she had struggled in life, I was able to open up and share my struggles. We then created a bond over our shortcomings. A bond that has bloomed into a great friendship.

We researched each other's lives then combined our interests together to see if they aligned. Then we decided if we could be friends. Since our paths matched so well, we were able to connect.

Another friend of mine is Ellen Vrana. She lives in London. One day out of the blue she messaged me and said something about how brave it was to share my own personal stories over the Internet. She said something about how it had encouraged her to share her own stories. I assume she had done countless hours of research on who I was as she brought up specific points in some stories I had shared. After she had done her research to see if our interests aligned, she reached out.

Since she was so nice when she reached out and did her research with me; we bonded. I helped promote her content when she started writing and guided more eyes to what she created. She lived up to creating what she had set out to do and we created a long term friendship. However, without that initial research on her end, I doubt our paths would have ever crossed. Which would be quite a shame because I really do enjoy our friendship together.

After you do your research of potential people whom you feel could be a part of your friend circle, reach out. Connect with them. Send them a nice kind message reflecting common ground. Address them by their name and start chatting. You have already overcome the first obstacle of finding a friend, sharing common ground. Move on to step two, creating a bond.

With all things in life, we won't be completely sure of what we get. These friendships may only last a few months but, if you're lucky, they could last until the rest of your life. With the potential of having a life-long friendship, wouldn't it be worth taking that risk of sending the first message?

LEONARD KIM

8 HOW TO INITIATE A CONVERSATION WITH A POTENTIAL BUSINESS ASSOCIATE OR CLIENT

Some of us who may be reading this book want to do more than just find a friend. We may want to expand our business.

When it comes to expanding a business, there are many things we can do. We can go out and search for customers or clients who can use our services. We can look for employees and business partners who can help us spread our message. We can also look for investors who can help fund our dreams.

When in a business setting, we might think etiquette becomes even more important than on a friendship level. This takes me back to a quote I remember renowned author John C. Maxwell once said: "There's no such thing as business ethics. There's only ethics."

We might get confused and think that etiquette in a business setting is different from etiquette in our everyday life, but it is not. It is the exact same thing.

Just like how ethics are the same whether in a business environment or not, etiquette is the same in and out of business situations. We can't separate something into a different category just because it involves business. Instead, they are one and the same.

Just like how we went out there and did research on our potential online friends, we have to do the same thing when conducting business. The people we do business with will be doing the exact same thing. Because of that, we need to look at every aspect that we already covered.

First is visibility. Our reputation has been on the line since day one when we started up our business. Actually, our reputation was on the line even before that. Our own name associates us with who we are and what we do. If our name has a bad reputation associated with it, then it doesn't matter what business we try to cover it up with. Have you cleaned up your social media and removed all forms of bad etiquette that may be lingering around? If you haven't, then anyone doing a Google search on the founding partners of the business may end up coming up with some dirt. Before initializing in any new conversations, clean up your social media.

As a refresher, next comes *be, do, have*. You need to make sure you are acting as a professional business owner. Sometimes this is easier said than done. People often mistake that to become successful, they may need to act cocky and arrogant. It's just the contrary. Instead, be humble, hungry, and honest with others.

Then comes personal etiquette. Make sure to be as civil as possible. There is no room for fights or arguments here because in today's society everything is documented. One wrong claim stated to the wrong person can permanently be imprinted onto the Internet for the world to see.

After we have covered our foundation, we need to figure out exactly what we are looking for:

- Clients.
- Business Partners.
- Investors.

We will be approaching all these people in a similar, yet different fashion.

Clients:

First we have to figure out who our ideal clients are. What are their interests? What do they want from our product? Why would they want it? Would it solve some of their existing problems? How will it benefit their lives?

Then we have to figure out how we want to approach these people. Do we want to have our company publicized in a media outlet? Do we want to reach out to customers individually? How should we go about doing this on the Internet?

Getting media coverage is hard. It also will not directly result in attaining any clients. Instead, the best way to get clients would be through engagement. In the sales funnel, there are two ways to generate clients. One is through outbound methods considered to be new business development. The other is through inbound methods considered to be marketing.

What is the difference?

Outbound methods would be to reach out to clients on an individual basis. To reach out and create a connection with a potential client. In the past, this was like cold calling. But with the Internet, social media, and forum sites everywhere, this has become much easier. It is no longer a cold call because with the proper research our customers are already telling us about their problems. We just need to connect the dots when we make our responses.

Inbound methods of marketing are more like setting up a blog or writing answers and solutions in help forums. People are facing problems every day. By creating a model where we educate our customers for free, we have a much higher chance of winning over paid clients.

Recently, I was on the market for a new day job. I signed up for a job site and submitted my resume to a few employers. As a bonus, they offered me a free evaluation of my resume. The person who had looked it over was thorough about what could have been better. Instead of fixing the mistakes myself, I paid this company their going rate of $189 to redo it.

I'm Asian. I don't like paying for anything. I save every penny I get. However, since this consultant took the time to be thorough during their free initial assessment, I was happy to pay for their services. If you offer free initial consultations to your potential clients you can turn them into paid clients.

Business Partners:

Rarely, people will approach us to help us in our business endeavors. We usually have to reach out to find the people we are looking for. We all know that we can't do it alone, but most of us try to anyway. That is, until we hit that bottleneck when we can no longer get any further.

I have hit that bottleneck many times. Usually it was because I did not have the programming knowledge and technical know-how of how to move forward. Since I have a background in marketing, programming has always been confusing for me. I am sure that programmers feel the same way about marketing. The problem lies in the fact that in order for there to be a successful company everyone has to work together.

This is where it gets difficult. In most situations, like friendships, all we have to do is like each other and have common interests. In partnership situations, the people we need will be unlike how we are. We all will have different skill sets that are essential, but we will have to learn how to work together.

Working with someone who has unique skill sets that you don't understand will be as hard as learning a new language. The only way to do it smoothly is to go back to the research phase. Understand as much about their craft as possible, then find other things to relate on. Maybe the ultimate goal for your company aligns to the interest of the programmer. This could help bridge the gap when there are no common interests between you two.

When you two find common ground within the goals of the company, you can work together on creating more common interests at work. This should help you start a trusting relationship together.

Investors:

Thousands of people are starting new businesses daily. Some people want money to fund a brick and mortar location. Others want money to start the next billion dollar technology business. Investors get messages all the time. They are some of the most sought after people on the Internet. What is going to distinguish you from all the other messages the investor receives?

That's simple.

Most of the people who are sending over their proposals forget about formalities. They aren't following the guide of etiquette. Nor are they doing any research on the investors they approach. They are taking their same business model and executive summary and sending it to every investment group they can find.

What if you could make a connection instead?

Let's say an angel investor had a blog where he showcased his seminars and speeches. If you had done your research and watched a few of his videos, would you have a better understanding of who he was? If you used what you had learned about him in a message, would it be more personal?

Your initial contact is meant to connect and engage, not to sell. Use that research to your advantage and connect with your investor. Ask him how he felt doing that seminar at UCLA. Or what he learned when he made the mistake of investing in Betterworks. Personalize your message.

What you don't want to do is send the same message to everyone. I'm not an investor, but I once received this generic message in my inbox.

> Hi Leonard,
> My name is [redacted],
>
> The reasons I contact you before others are that, first I really like your Quora posts and it seems like you have an interesting life, and secondly you are experienced in startups and marketing.
>
> [redacted] is a startup for me (I want to expand into a business when time and funds come), and it is an iOS app for social media marketing.
>
> What the app does (I won't go into abysmal details), is that you get more followers or likes for your Twitter and Instagram accounts, and Facebook pages.
>
> I saw that you have a Facebook page (let me check if you have Twitter or Instagram too), please try [redacted[to get more likes for your Facebook page. Then, if you are interested, tell me if you like the idea of it, what can be improved, and if you are interested in investing in the app (I can offer equity or pay you back).
>
> Sincerely,
> [redacted]

In his message, he was asking for an investment. I use tracking tools on my content. At the time I had received this message, this person had only read one piece of my content, which was a date that had gone wrong. It had nothing to do with any of my business experience, yet he acted as if he had read my business content. If he did, he should have stated what he read and how it related to him and made a true connection. If he had read further, he would have seen that I was not an accredited investor. Then he wouldn't have had to waste his time sending me a message.

This brings us to the most important part of how to start a conversation with any type of business associate.

One main problems that I have seen throughout all business transactions is the lack of human exchange. Most people write in a business tone when they are conducting business, leaving out their personality. They write in pure business speak, where we are unable to get a sense of their personality at all.

In order for your clients, business partners, and investors to connect with you, they need to get a sense for your personality. Don't hide your personality under layers of business speak. Let yourself shine through your words. It may be the determining factor that will help you secure your new deals!

9 HOW TO SEEK OUT A MENTOR OR ASK FOR ADVICE

Sometimes in life, we just get stuck. We encounter a stage where we don't know what to do.

Other times, we want to move forward. We want to improve our network and surround ourselves with people whom we would like to learn from. Or we would like experts to check our work and verify that the people we are working with are doing what they said they would do.

Whenever we encounter either of these situations what we often do next is look for a mentor. A mentor who can either help us overcome immediate obstacles or one who will be able to help guide us in the future.

When looking for a mentor it is important to be picky. But we also have to understand that mentors are busy and cannot be there for us at every whim. Finding a mentor is simple early in life, but gets much harder as we age. As each day passes, we gain more skills, so the pools of mentors who can help us get better shrink.

What I like to look for in a mentor is life experience. What have they done in their life? Are they honest? Do they have ethics? Are they an expert in their field? Have they worked as an expat? Have they traveled the world? What kind of jobs did they have? Have they sold companies? What kind of failures did they experience? How did they handle certain situations?

All these are questions that I seek the answers for before even contacting a mentor. My personal mentor is a man by the name of James Altucher, best-selling author of the books *Choose Yourself* and *The Power of No*. When I had discovered his content for the first time, I locked on to him. I started to read everything that he had written. What he wrote was so thought provoking that while I was doing my research on him, I was learning at the same time.

Most busy people have a defense mechanism to weed out the people who contact them. According to Altucher's book, before initiating a conversation with someone, he says no three times. Little did I know, that when I had first contacted him, I was following his process of how to turn a no into a yes.

In the fall of 2013 I had hit a phase where my life was changing. I was a nobody, but I saw that my marketing and branding efforts had paid off. I laid out the foundation and I was slowly becoming a somebody. I take that back. I was rapidly becoming a public figure. I was trying to balance full time school, full time work, and managing my brand. It was too much for me to handle.

I had sent James Altucher a long-winded message begging for help on how to handle the situation. That was a mistake. It was 17 paragraphs long. No one has that much time to read anything. Instead, what I would recommend for you to do when sending a message to your mentor is to keep it short. Three paragraphs would be ideal.

Most mentors will not respond on the first outreach. Yet, most people save and archive their emails. If you reach out, over and over, one day they will respond. Stay consistent and follow up if you don't hear a response. I did that by tagging James Altucher in other social media posts and writing content based around his philosophies.

After staying on Altucher's radar, he recognized me for the first time. He upvoted some of my content on Quora, then later proceeded to add me as a friend on Facebook. Before the end of 2013, we had a minor conversation on Facebook. I was shocked. He actually responded to my messages. I jumped for joy like a little school girl. Then in April of 2014, I flew out to New York, where I was able to meet James and his wife Claudia Altucher for breakfast at the W Hotel in Times Square.

It is kind of unreal, to be able to meet someone whom I looked up to at such a critical moment in my life. Someone whom I considered to be a mentor. He is the only person whom I can think of that has gone through more hardships than I have yet made it out unscathed. What is even more surprising is how philanthropic of a person James Altucher is. I have nothing that I could ever offer him, yet he still decided to act as my mentor.

However, sometimes we need to give in order to take.

Other mentors of ours may see us as their mentors as well. My friend James Liu, founder of BoxCat Games, says that through my life experiences, I remind him of his father. When he needs help with the marketing, operations, or contracts for his business, he knows he is more than welcome to come to me.

James Liu managed teams that created technology. The kind of technology that helped track down serial killers and ensure voters couldn't rig elections. When I need help with figuring out if a programmer is doing their job correctly, I go to him. We both see each other as thought leaders in our specific fields. By providing each other advice, we have created a win-win scenario.

Another mentor of mine is a friend whom I went to high school with. His name is Neil Patel. He owns Kissmetrics and writes marketing advice on a blog called Quicksprout. Coincidentally, we both sold burnt CDs in high school and worked at Knott's Berry

Farm doing park services as our first job. We started out our real world experience by getting into sales. Then we migrated into a profession where we were picking up trash, bussing tables and cleaning restrooms. Luckily, since have a warm connection and went to school together, it is much easier for me to get in contact with him.

So what do we do when we reach out to a mentor? We connect, relate, and engage. Then continue to follow up at various internals until we have a response.

I first read James Altucher's content on April 10, 2013. I reached out on September 4, 2013. We first talked on December 29, 2013 at 9:46 a.m. We first met on April 18, 2014. It takes time to connect, but if you show determination and sincerity, you will eventually connect. Keep trying. It will be well worth it in the end.

10 NASTY PEOPLE. TOXICITY AND ITS DOWNSIDES

Let's face it, in the world there are a lot of rude people. Some are even bullies. They want to say things that stir us up inside. I have millions of views on my content on the Internet, so I see a lot of comments that make me mad. Like the average person, when someone verbally attacks me, I want to do either one of two things: I want to either stick my head under the ground and bury it like an ostrich or lash out and take all my anger out on the person who wrote the comment.

Throughout the Internet, we will even see blog posts that are just toxic in nature. Full of hate to the world. Some will disgust us so bad that we will want to comment. Other times, we might find something so offensive that we want to lash out at the author.

Then we might encounter the ultimate death trap, trolls.

Now, you might be asking: what exactly is a troll?

According to Wikipedia, a troll is "a person who sows discord on the Internet by starting arguments or upsetting people, by posting inflammatory, extraneous, or off-topic messages in an online community (such as a newsgroup, forum, chat room, or blog) with the deliberate intent of provoking readers into an emotional response or of otherwise disrupting normal on-topic discussion." [4]

In other words, a troll is an online bully whose only purpose in life is to ruin your day.

The ultimate goal of a troll is to rile us up. They say things with one intent. To anger us. To get our blood boiling. To make us lose composure.

When we react out of character, the troll is overjoyed. We try to respond in a sensible non manic way, but our blood is boiling. They are laughing as they write their next comment, that infuriates us even more.

Ha. Ha. Ha. Ha. Ha.

This is what is going through the mind of the troll, who is just a 15-year-old kid in high school with nothing better to do with their time. They're sitting in class sharing your responses with their friends. They all gather around and laugh together.

They will do whatever they can do, attack our beliefs, our religions, our political parties, or even our families. There is no line that is too far for the troll to cross. They don't see you as a human. They have dehumanized you into a tool for their enjoyment. A tool that they can rile up and humiliate, without any recourse at all.

The downsides of reacting negatively can be detrimental to our image. Remember, we want to maintain our etiquette. Joining in with the troll and attacking back will not only leave you feeling like a fool, but will allow the troll to win. They will have succeeded at helping you harm your own reputation, by making you lose focus and reply with your emotions.

[4] http://en.wikipedia.org/wiki/Troll_(Internet)

When you look outraged in that one moment on the Internet, you look like a person who is unreliable. Someone who is hot-tempered and easy to get to react to things. Someone who doesn't think before they act. I know this because I have encountered it myself. In my day, we didn't have a guide that told us what we should or shouldn't do on the Internet. I had to learn from my own experience.

In my own experience, when I was originally attacked by trolls, I fought back. Then I fought back some more. I may have won a few arguments here and there. However, if I went back to a conversation three months into the future, I realized that I just looked like a complete moron. If an employer had looked over a discussion I had, then they would see me as a loose cannon. Only through time and experience, did I realize that engaging in negative behavior online was a very bad thing to do. But with that experience, I am able to share with you the toxicity and the downsides that come with the reactions.

11 THE IMPORTANCE OF SELF-CONTROL AND ZEN STUFF

After encountering so much negativity on the Internet and realizing that I looked like a fool, I had to take a step back. I reflected upon on the importance of self-control. No matter how bad we want things in life, as humans, we need to exercise self-control. If we eat each piece of candy that we see, we might end up with cavities. If we eat all the food around us, we might gain weight and become a glutton. If we try to take every dollar we can get, we might end up in some unethical situations. If we try to cheat on some tests, our morals may be compromised. One day we may one day end up stealing, or worse.

The same goes for responding to situations on the Internet. When the trolls attack, we need to impose self-control. We need to get in touch with our inner zen and stay calm. If we let our emotions control our decisions, then we will look stupid. One of the main goals of exercising the etiquette of social media is to avoid looking stupid.

Remember, the troll is a 15-year-old high school kid. Would you belittle yourself to enter into an argument with someone whose only purpose in life is to rile you up? To get you to continue to express your points? Someone who doesn't care what you have to say, but only wants to attack you again?

Trolls are playing a game. A game that you cannot win. When you are facing a situation that you cannot win, the best thing to do is to not respond at all. Instead, get in touch with your inner zen.

Did you just encounter a nasty comment on something you wrote? It is going to be okay. Stay calm. Take a deep breath. Hold for five seconds. Release for ten. Repeat this breathing exercise ten times. It will help lower your heart rate to bring your mind back to a calm state. If that isn't working, when you start feeling angry, snap a rubber band on your wrist. The pain will help interrupt the pattern of anger to distract you.

After you have done this, the next best thing to do would be to enter the kitchen. Get out your favorite tea pot or kettle. If you don't have one, go buy one. Then boil some water. Pour it into a ceramic cup. Dabble in a few drops of your tea bag. I like the ones that bloom flowers. They're pretty. After the tea settles, sip slowly. Use the next thirty minutes to enjoy a peaceful environment where you can just become one with your tea. Personally, I like the taste of green tea, but all teas will work great in this situation. If it is nighttime, chamomile tea will help you sleep. Sleep is a great way to get in touch with your soul while you forget about the toxic comments you received.

I hate to say this, because I believe that we are all equals in life. No one is better than anyone else. We are all terminals, transmitting data and learning from each other. But in this particular situation, things are different. This is a battlefield where your enemy has one goal, to destroy you. You are better than the troll. Don't stoop down to their level. Stay calm and true to yourself. Your soul, along with your reputation, will thank you when it's over.

12 HOW TO RESPOND TO NASTY COMMENTS

Now that you have had time to relax, you have to make a decision. The troll left a comment. You can either leave it there, which is the recommended route, or you can respond.

If you choose to respond, the best way to do this is to disassociate the attack from yourself. Don't take anything anyone says on the Internet personally. They don't know you. They never will. You won't ever have them over for tea in your quiet time. Why let them into your mind? They don't deserve to be there.

The most mature thing to do is to not acknowledge that the comments are even there. In just under a year, I had five million views on my content. With being such a highly visible person, I was under attack from all angles. Some people just wanted to rip into me. Some people condemned what I had written. Other people just wanted to mock me.

Most of the time, I did the right thing. I ignored those comments. However, sometimes one of these comments would catch me off guard. Then I'd react. After failing to react in the right way so many times, I have figured out how to respond properly.

Let's say someone says something like this to you:

John Doe: "Your writing is horrible. I can't believe that they even let you write or publish anything on the Internet."

Be as kind as possible.

"John, this is valuable information. Thank you so much for your incredible feedback. I have always been looking for someone with as sharp as an eye as yours to critique my work. One day, my goal is to become a great writer. I will not be able to do that without the help of critics who demand perfection, like you in my life. Will you please help me by identifying what portions of my post are causing me to disconnect with my audience? I would love to either discuss this over phone or email. Can we please discuss this further? I'll bring the crumpets and tea!"

Or if they say this:

Jane Doe: "I could make something look better by tossing piles of poop at the wall."

"Jane, I love your artistic sense of humor. You had me at tossing. I wish I could have the wit to make jokes like you. You must think that what I had written had some problems. Can you please identify exactly where the problem is? I'm new at this writing thing. I would love to get all the help I can to make worthwhile content. I want the people who read my stuff to feel happy. How can I make you feel happy? Would you like a hug?"

If you share love, in some instances you will get love in return. Or you may not get any message back at all. Sometimes, people don't see other users as people on the Internet. They just see words on a screen and feel like they can act any way they want. But, once they encounter a reaction like this, they will get shocked. They might simply disappear because they only wanted to troll you. Or they might apologize and provide the valuable feedback you need to improve your writing skills. Either way, you win.

On extremely rare occasions, you may end up as a victim to cyber bullying. Sometimes, there is a group of people will gang up on you, with the intent to publicly humiliate you. If this ever happens, document and save the conversation. Go to your local authorities, whether it be your principal at school, an administrator of a website, or if the threat is serious, then the officers of the law and report the incident. Then block all communication with the other users. Whatever you do, do not engage. These people are out for blood and will do anything to put you down.

13 TIPS TO A HAPPY LIFESTYLE, LIKE DRINKING TEA AND HAPPY RELATIONSHIPS

Just like our homes, the Internet should be a happy place. It should be a place where we are comfortable to share what we feel. A place where we get along with other people and make friends and business connections.

Since I was fourteen, I have been on the Internet. Being a teenage boy, I originally used the resource to find girls. I used to go in chatrooms on AOL (America On-Line) and message every single woman I could find. Before etiquette existed, we sent message that said "a/s/l". This led to the beginning of our conversations. I am pretty sure I found my first girlfriend this way.

As time progressed, I started to message girls on a website called Findapix. This was back when I was actually good with girls. I met hundreds upon hundreds of women on that website. But not everyone whom I met was normal. One girl I had met grew chickens in her back yard. I slept over one day. The next morning, I heard a chicken scream. The poor bird was being served for dinner. Another time, this import model tried to force me to eat chicken feet. Even though she was voluptuous, this led to our breakup. Then one day Findapix ceased to exist. So did my luck with women.

Now I use the Internet to share the insights of what I have learned throughout the last few decades of my life.

The Internet is a huge resource that we will have for the rest of our lives, unless something even better replaces it. It is no longer just a tool for the privileged, but a way of life for each one of us. Since it is a tool that we will have to use for the rest of our lives, learning the values of etiquette in this book will be absolutely essential for the success of your life.

But we can't forget what else is important to us. Our real life friends are just as important, if not more important than our online friends. Just because we are making an online presence and creating friends on forums and social media platforms, we can't neglect our real life friends. Remember that we still have to live a happy life. To live a happy life, we have to invest in all our relationships, both online and offline. Make sure to frequently share moments of zen with your friends as you drink tea in peace. When you're out and about, you are more than welcome to share your Internet adventures with your friends. They will in turns share theirs with you.

We are as intertwined with technology now as we once were with our phones. But just remember, the Internet is not our lives. Social media is not our lives. Our lives consist of what we do outside of the Internet. What we do for work and where we go out with our friends. So invest heavily into those relationships. For us, the Internet is nothing more than a tool. A tool that will allow you to connect with others everywhere, whether they are across the street or halfway across the world from you. But most importantly, be happy.

The key to happy relationships is keeping in touch. Asking your friends how their day went. Being genuinely interested in what they have to say. Having an open mind with a sense of curiosity will keep you at the forefront of happiness.

Then comes the most important part. Do not create expectations in any of your relationships. Just enjoy their company. Without expectation, there is no disappointment. With expectation, things can go wrong. Then when they do, we will feel miserable. Much like how we are unable to predict what will happen tomorrow, we should not expect anyone to do anything that we think they would. Instead, we should just hope for the best and live each day to the fullest. Rely on yourself, for at the end of the day, you will be the only person you can count on.

LEONARD KIM

14 CONCLUSION: START CONNECTING TODAY

Thank you so much for taking this journey through the etiquette of social media with me. I commend you for sticking it through the whole journey. Now you have all the tools that you need to make sure you share your thoughts in an eloquent manner.

Want to connect with a new friend? Have an important person you need to reach out to? Have a fight arising in the horizon?

You are now equipped with the thought process of exactly what to do in each of these situations.

Today is the day. I bid you to take action. Connect. Go out there and make a friend. Try these new concepts and put them into action. Create a new friendship. Start a new business relationship. Get yourself prepared for college applications or a new job.

Within a year, by following the methods that I have shared in this book, I went from being someone that nobody wanted anything to do with to a person that people from all across the world come to for advice. The funny thing is that I didn't change what type of person I am.

All I did was change my form of etiquette. If I could make these kind of changes in my life, imagine what you could do in yours as well.

Just even the slightest steps forward can create a ripple effect. If you are able to handle a situation online eloquently, someone of significance may notice. They may share that deed with others. It could potentially be heard by employers, who want to seek you out for a job. Imagine if something like that were to happen for you.

Life works in mysterious ways. We reap what we sow. Everything we do comes back to us, sometimes when we least expect it. Go out there and spread those seeds of etiquette today. One day, your fields will harvest and you will reap the rewards.

Take this journey with me. When you do, I will promise you one thing.

That promise you ask?

You will not regret it.

15 BONUS CHAPTER: DON'T BE AWKWARD

On July 5, 2014, I went to Cantalini's Salerno Beach Restaurant in Los Angeles. I met with my friends Terrence Yang and Vivy Chao of Yang Ventures for dinner. We were having a blast, discussing all the random messages we get on the Internet. As requested by Terrence, I will be providing some insights on what not to do when messaging someone on the Internet. I will share them here with you too.

The media tells us to be ourselves.

If you are an antisocial person who is like a programmer, that can be quite difficult to do. When we are ourselves, we hide in a shell and peek out like a turtle. That doesn't work when we are trying to communicate.

Other people are just weird. I'm one of them. People like me end up saying whatever comes to our mind and send off a message that makes no sense. So I have to pay close attention to what I am writing before I click that "Send" button.

Since the lines are not black and white about what we can or cannot do, I will be providing some examples of what *not* to do when on the Internet. These kinds of things will make you look awkward and unusual. People may end up questioning what type of person you are. That may end up costing you potential friendships or business deals.

Here are some examples of messages that I have never responded to within my inbox:

Hey there Leo! (I hope I can call you that..) What are the Job descriptions of Each of your titles on your Bio line?

This person gives me a nickname and acts like we're in a job interview. Yet he initiated the conversation.

Hey Leonard,I need your Help ASAP ! :D

The sense of urgency in this message made sure I didn't respond. I'm a busy person. I can't work on a stranger's time schedule.

How do you have so much time to spend on Quora? You answer a lot, you're online all the time, interact with everyone who interacts with you, How's that? Are you the Batman :P ?

It sounds like the message was sent in a playful tone, but I took it offensively.

Hi Leonard
Ive been reading your views since an hour and a half
..really great...I am inspired..though I havnt had as many hardahips as uve had....yet for d little bad tyms ive seen.....I feel good bout it Glad!

Great message, poor grammar. I simply cannot respond to that.

Hi Leonard,

If you happen to see my message can you please call me on
+xxxxxxxxx404

As I am unsure of what I want from life. By profession I am a
Project Manager.

Why would I call anybody?!?

You know what? Your story is just... I don't know. Let's talk -
xxxxx@gmail.com

What would we talk about?!?!

Upvote my posts please I need urgent credits.
The tale of the burned.

Thank you.

No warm welcome?!

Hi,
I have a request. Could you please send me some credits from your
pool of oh-so-many credits?

He should just hold out his hand in front of 7-Eleven. Better yet,
hold out a tin can.

Are you tall? Saw someone like you walking in Boston, but it was a
tall man and... ..IDK.

Thanks

I don't even live anywhere near Boston. But this guy doesn't
even bother to say hi!

I don't know if this is your area of interest, but I would really
appreciate if you could provide some views on this: Master's in
Computer Science: What are the Effects of Resigning from a class
during MS?

It surely isn't my area of interest, which he could have found out if he did his research.

Sir i dont know who u r ...but i m suffering from that same phase which u had when ur girlfriend left
she is in my college
i waited for 8 long months of silence to listen her saying i love u to me
6 mnths down the line...we just fought over a little matter and left me alone
i still remember her..d*** it..i still love her
i dont know whether she even remembers me or not
i heard it from one of my friend that she hates me
i had proposals from 3 other girls..and i said no to all of them
coz i still love her...i cant see her in distress ..like if she sees me wid other grls ..what will she think ??..and blah blah blah..
so i now ignore girls and dnt talk to them
the most amazing thing is when one of my friends asked her whether she found another guy...to that she replied-"i still respect my ex..i cant see him in pain..the pain he will have when he sees me wid sm1 else"
what do i do after this
plzz any suggestion...i would love to have it
plzz sir..help me..a little time of yours can change my life

This person sent each line as an individual message. He scared me away. Plus the grammar...

We are a company based out in [xyz] working on different technologies in [abc]. We have developed few innovative concepts for Mobile as well as Web.

Have had a chance to look at your profile which creates an interest for me, is there any opportunity we can get connected through right mean of Skype, if we can help each other?

My Skype ID is [redacted]

Looking forward to your response.

Person

This person didn't even try to connect nor introduce himself. He went straight in for the kill without building common ground first.

Are you a bot ?
How else can you vote up a comment so quickly ?

It's always great to start a conversation with an insult.

Just wanted to say you look like Bruce lee!

How I look has absolutely nothing to do with anything.

Hi, you answered a question about writing b-plan. You used a mind map in the answer but the picture there is not clear. Can you send me the link to that picture

He is asking me for a favor, but he didn't use my name or say please or thank you.

This one particular person is extremely awkward in many of the messages he has sent me. He says he has an IQ of 150. Here are a few examples:

Do you have an erotic personality? [xyz] said you're needy in a good way.

Personally I'm kind of super independent and don't really need to talk to other people and I've never really felt an inclination to 'find someone' to be with romantically.

That sounds like an insult. Awkward!

But all your posts about women are about the ones you misjudge.

Like that girl that you thought was a gold digger but wasn't.

He assumes everything I do is an error in judgment, by creating a blanket statement over what I write about.

when did you become yoda?

What in the world is this even supposed to mean?

Also, it is probably a good idea to never mention your IQ. It can be seen as bragging.

Here are some examples of some conversations I had that were absolutely weird:

Once I had a conversation with this fellow:

Person: "I will just say I got my a** chewed) All of which was deleted and I was promptly blocked. I plan to speak with Quora investors and get these issues fixed"

Leonard Kim: "I see."

Person: "I am going to bring it up at Stanford, because its unlikely quora will serve their investors by fixing this issue"

Leonard Kim: "What's the crown? I didn't see the crown on any profiles (but i haven't been looking, have been taking a break from quora the last week)."

Person: "its that quill and ink put symbol in the upper left of a profile. many I know got one"

Leonard Kim: "Oh, that's to represent top writer 2013 I think. It's just some promo feel good type thing or something issued by the site to I guess reward people who contribute a lot?"

Person: "yes, but there are some bad apples"

Leonard Kim: "There are, you're right. A handful of them."

As you can see from our chat log, I have absolutely no clue what this guy is talking about. He just goes off ranting like I even have the slightest idea of what he is saying. He doesn't even try to catch my

THE ETIQUETTE OF SOCIAL MEDIA

attention with any points. I end up having zero interest in what he
has to say.

A few months after, I wrote an article on angel investors. I
discussed how I met with Terrence. I put it up on LinkedIn.

He then commented:

"I found both you and Terrance have a bit of a bubble to discussion,
even when you know I am an established Investor, I have never seen
either of you in the Valley and I have met almost everyone) Time
and opportunity don't always come within your terms. Telling
someone i don't want to talk to you anymore unless we talk about
what I want , or when or how isn't a way to build a relationship"

From my conversation that I had with him above, I had
absolutely no clue he was an investor. I thought he just wanted to
complain about things. Then later, he went off to spell Terrence's
name wrong and insulted both of us by saying we're unapproachable.
But did you see that message he sent me?

Another awkward situation was this:

Person: "Hey Leonard. It's Michael. Hey, I was hoping to capitalize
off your popularity via a response... :(. We can help each out. We
both get credits if you respond. It would be much appreciated!!!"

Leonard Kim: "Oh. It was a lame question."

Person: "Ok. Sure. You're right. Next time, then.Although. I think
saying it was a lame question as a response would be great too :p.
Sincerity is awesome!!!"

Leonard Kim: "K"

He showed that he was greedy. I mean that was bad, but not as
bad as what happened next.

Person: "So Leonard. I've concluded that you are a bot or are
multiple people. Is this correct? Probably a combination of both.

That's right. I'm calling you out. Refutation? I don't mind. I just want to know the motivation for the experiment. So are you actually admitting to being a bot/ multiple accounter for real or no?"

Then he tried to defame me publicly as well. That was an interesting situation that publicly made him look like a fool.

Person: "you are awesome ! i want to talk to you. can you please give me you email id ? i know you are too busy"

Leonard Kim: "Thanks! Seek and ye shall find."

Person: "you mail address ?"

Person (five days later): "?"

This person wanted to collect my email address so he could reach out to me.

He missed an essential step in the etiquette of social media. He forgot to do his research. My email is listed on my profile page. If he had taken two minutes to look for it, he would have been able to send me the message he wanted to send.

Person: "Hi Leonard, Thank you for following back. I am looking for mentor. Will you be able to help?"

Leonard Kim: "What are you working on?"

Person: "For Startup help and Life Coach! Can you help Leo?"

Person (several weeks later): "Hello Leo, Hope you are doing well. I am just following up on my request of last month. Will you be able to help?"

Leonard Kim: "What are you working on?"

This person completely ignored my question.

THE ETIQUETTE OF SOCIAL MEDIA

Person: "How about we change effectively the world, for once?
I bring the strategy based on the "obvious" (a cant loose strategy)!
you bring the money? Not enough? Ok, you are a tough guy...if
(THE BIG IF)you bring any material or tangible means I demand for
whenever I want, I'll give you this strategy, all the credits and the
fame and whatever and the key to integrally become The Sole
Strategist (yes, don't count me) in the world.
So...we have a deal? or do you think I'm delusional?

Leonard Kim: "I don't understand."

Person: "And what do you want me to do? to change the format of
my writing? To understand for you? I made myself pretty clear in an
entertaining and funny way but none the less clear."

Leonard Kim: "What's your idea?"

Person: "have you got the means?"

Leonard Kim: "I don't know what it is."

Person: "money for logistics"

I still have absolutely no clue what this guy was talking about. He
did ask me if I thought he was delusional though. I will have to say
that I feel that he is.

Person: "Morning. I'm working on a consumer Internet company and
I need to hit traction so I can raise cash to hire and to acquire and
retain market share. Any advice?"

Leonard Kim: "Hello Mr. [xyz]. Possibly. However that's too vague
to go off of."

Person: "Ok."

He says no to himself when I didn't. He doesn't even try to
explain his idea. He limits himself from his own success.

Person: "Hey! I don't know you and its obvious... May I know where do you practically work at/ work for ?"

Leonard Kim: "What do you mean?"

Person: "I meant I tried to google you but didn't find a result... Where do you work/ which company do you work for ?"

Leonard Kim: "Don't I have it in my profile?"

Person: "'Corporate Strategist', it says, but not exactly...a corporate strategist of which company ?I'm sorry I didn't mean to be rude"

Person: "Oops! I had been so ignorant about you Kim! Apologies... I mean *'Leonard Kim'"

Why is this person so hung up on where I work?

Person: "Do you have desires to want to help the trafficking victim?"

Leonard Kim: "What did you have in mind?"

Person: "Well I am someone who have been degraded and raped in [xyz]. Arent u aware of this? If not dont u want to get involved?"

Leonard Kim: "I'm sorry to hear that. I'm aware of it. Involved in which way?"

Person: "Well do u feel moral duty to want to help a rape victim?"

Leonard Kim: "One specific victim or a group?"

Person: "Well I am sure there are more victims in [xyz] other than myself. But whether or not they like to claim themselves as victims of crime is totally different matter. Are you a korean american person from [abc]? Do you recognize my face by any chance? Because I lived in [xyz] for many years."

Leonard Kim: "I don't recognize your face but yes. I am Korean American. I read some of your material. That must've really sucked. If you want financial help, I don't have money. If you had something else in mind, I'm open to options."

Person: "Do u want to chat on skype or kakao talk?"

Leonard Kim: "Maybe after I do this mud mask, shower and eat. I already put the mud mask on."

Person: "Ok. I meant chatting in text format. Whenenver you are ready. I might fall asleep anyway but my userid is [redacted] for kakao talk."

Leonard Kim: "I don't have KakaoTalk. It's not available for my BlackBerry."

Person: "Do u have skype on blackberry? What is your bloodtype and how do u personally feel about woman who has been sexually exploited personally?"

Leonard Kim: "I have Skype on my computer. I don't know my blood type. sometimes I care. I guess, indifferent? I don't know. I never really thought of it."

Person: "Skype or here its not important I suppose. How do you feel about the scupture of a korean girl who were used as sex slave by japanese army in glendale ca? Are you also in favor of marijuana legalization?"

Leonard Kim: "I didn't see the sculpture. I don't watch the news. I don't smoke marijuana so it doesn't affect me."

During this whole conversation, I felt like this person was pushing me back into a wall. I didn't even know what to do. Why did she want to know what my blood type was? It was so confusing to me.

Person: "You passed answering both the questions. But I asked you first because it is fun to read your answers. More than fun, I enjoy reading your answers."

Leonard Kim: "I don't know anything about mobile technology and I don't really watch sports."

Person: "That's okay. I will keep asking you to answer all my questions. Hopefully I get an answer from you for any of my questions :) Anyway thanks."

Leonard Kim: "You can ask me life questions or business questions and I'll answer them. I don't know much else."

Person: "I'm still a student whose doing my Bachelors in Business Management. So I really don't have any questions related to business. If there is any questions related to life, I will inbox you because sometimes I'm not comfortable asking publicly as I am scared that people might judge."

Leonard Kim: "Okay."

Person: "Thank you for your time for replying to my messages."

Leonard Kim: "Oh you're welcome [person]. Thanks for thinking I'm smarter than I am in being able to potentially answer your questions."

This person just wants to continually pester and annoy me, even though I don't have any domain knowledge in the categories he asks me questions in.

Person: "Hello Leo .. I am a young businessman looking for immediate success instead of taking a traditional route to college. I was wondering if we could become connected & perhaps I will be able to ask you some questions? Any reply is appreciated .. I do have Twitter & plan on expanding my social media image progressively through time, although I plan to establish myself primarily .."

Leonard Kim: "What does immediate success mean?"

Person: "Occurring or accomplished without delay, instant; an immediate reply .. Literally, "overnight success," which I don't expect to be overnight but rather .. Day In, Day Out in an attempt to succeed overnight."

Leonard Kim: "There's no such thing as "immediate" success, unless you get lucky."

This person was living delusions of grandeur. That immediately turned me off from continuing the conversation.

Much like how you shouldn't touch a stranger's hair in real life, to recap, these are the things that you shouldn't do:

- Send a message without acknowledging the recipient by name.

- Give people nicknames without permission.

- Use poor grammar or textspeak.

- Make assumptions.

- Issue back handed compliments.

- Be condescending.

- Talk about how you are better than someone else.

- Tell people who they look like.

- Create a sense of urgency.

- Message people without researching who they are or where they work.

- Refusing to research how to contact someone, especially if it is on their bio.

- Rant about nonsense.

- Make accusations about how a person is without getting to know them

- Demand that someone stand behind your cause.

- Push people into corners.

- Ask irrelevant questions.

- Knowingly waste people's time.

- State that you want to capitalize off of someone else's efforts.

- Ignore direct questions.

- Continually send messages every few seconds as opposed to compiling them together as one.

- Talk about delusions of grandeur, like becoming an overnight success.

- Ask people if they think you are delusional.

- Vaguely describe your company and asking to connect, without first creating common ground.

- Refusing to provide more details when requested.

- Saying no to yourself when others are asking for clarification.

- Ask strangers to call or email you without connecting first.

- Ask people vague questions that they can research on their own.

- Ask for a favor without offering your services in return.

- Ask for handouts.

- Talk about how smart you are or how high your IQ is.

Thank you so much for taking the time to learn more about the etiquette of social media. Now that you know what not to do, you will be able to help prevent joy at your expense. You will now be able to avoid being laughed at and mocked while others are enjoying a fine Italian dinner in the heart of Playa Del Rey.

And as an additional bonus, here are a few messages that resonated well with me and engaged me to respond:

Hi Leonard,

I read your story and love your genuine response. It takes a lot of courage to reveal the ups and downs in life in such detail, and I really enjoy reading your post, for I can relate to my own life journey; my corporate and personal life's starting to crumble from the top.

During my professional work life, I learned that every email / message should close with an action item. While for this message I just want to say thank you – I will learn to live the life as an experience.

Best,
Person

This person did exactly what any person who wants to initiate a relationship online should do. He complimented me. Then he connected with me as he found our common ground. Had he made a request to speak further, I would have responded.

"Leonard, hope you're doing well!

I've been coming across your posts on Quora for some time, and just reading them has been fascinating. So although you don't know me, I was wondering if you might be in the LA area this coming weekend and would like to meet up sometime over coffee. (Though I work in New York now, I grew up in Cerritos and will be headed home for Thanksgiving!)

Most of all I'd like to just get a chance to meet you, but a small part of it is I'd also like to discuss with you your thoughts on business, entrepreneurship, personal development, investment, etc. I feel like I'm at a turning point in my life where I'd like to strike out on my own to do my own thing after following a straight-and-narrow course up to this point (exactly what that thing is yet, I don't know!), and would love to get the chance to talk to you about your experience.

Completely understand if the answer is no -- realize this could very well be the oddest Quora message you've ever received! At any rate, hope you have a happy holiday!

Best,
Jason Chen"

My response was as follows:

"Jason,

I've always wanted to be asked on a date. I just never knew it would be by a guy over the Internet. Would've much preferred a nice and lovely woman. However, I guess I can settle for a close second. I kid.

Sure, I can meet in LA. Don't set your expectations too high. I'm not nearly as smart as I sound."

The follow-up:

Jason: "Haha don't get your hopes up too, I'm not as good looking as I might sound! Would Saturday afternoon work for you? I can meet you anywhere in LA, just let me know what works."

Jason works at a private equity fund in New York. He used to work at McKinsey and Co. as a consultant out in Taiwan. Before that, he graduated from Stanford and Wharton. However, since he didn't have a profile picture nor a biography attached on the site, I was unaware of any of that.

Based solely on his initial message, we met In Los Angeles around Thanksgiving of 2013. In person, we connected and became friends. Then in April of 2014, I went to visit him in New York. Prior to going out to New York, he even offered to invest capital into a company I once wanted to run.

By complimenting me and stating that he valued my opinion when it came to business, I was compelled to meet him. His added humor was a plus to help win me over.

Hi Leonard,

Yesterday I was reading Quora before I was going to bed. What was supposed to be a light read ended up being an insightful read of many of your posts.

I was truly inspired by what you have gone through and I'll always look to some of your posts for inspiration when I'm questioning what am I doing in this world.

I hope to be able to stay in touch, as I feel any advice from you would be so much more valuable to me, than the generic advice I keep getting from the people around me.

Even though you have experienced so much, you have reached a state of gratitude and have a sense of purpose. I know for sure, you will continue to inspire people and may you reach the happiness you deserve.

God Bless Leonard!

If this person had ever decided to reach out to me for anything, I am pretty certain I wouldn't hesitate to respond.

Hey Leonard!

I just went through some of your answers on Quora, and found them heart warmingly brilliant.

You've indeed had a very interesting life and some ups and downs, but I love how you see the positivity of it all and have emerged as a better person.

It's been enlightening to read your answers. You're a man of strong grit and determination. I admire that immensely. :)

Agratha Dinakaran

This initial message was the beginning point of a friendship. If she had shaped her message in any other way, I may not have been inspired to meet her when she had visited Los Angeles from her country.

As we can see, there is a pattern to the successful messages that garner responses.

What are the common denominators of these successful messages?

Here, I'll help break them down for you. To recap on the etiquette of social media, these are what create a successful interaction:

- Grammar is properly used.

- Everyone addresses the respondent by name.

- Each message has a unique sense of personality, reflecting the messenger.

- A heartfelt and genuine compliment is stated at the beginning.

- All messengers work their way into building common ground on points which the respondent can relate, based on their initial research.

- They tell me the respondent that they respect and value their time.

- They provide the reason behind their message.

Learn from their messages and work on compiling your own. Remember, make your messages personal. Now go out there, have fun, and make friends!

I would love to hear about how this book has helped you in your life. Make sure to reach out to me and let me know how *The Etiquette of Social Media* has influenced your life!

ABOUT THE AUTHOR

Leonard Kim lives with his mother in Los Angeles. A business professional turned writer, he has shared his life experience to help the lives of others. By once having everything one could ever desire to losing it all, he has acquired extensive knowledge about essential life skills and effective communication. Through his musings, he was named a Top Writer on Quora, an Alexa ranked top 300 global website with a focus on sharing knowledge and advice.

Leonard's foundation lies in his ability to instill and reinforce racial and social equilibrium in an ever changing and progressive world.

He blogs at www.LeonardKim.com.

The best way to reach Leonard is by email: hello@leonardkim.com

Oh and he likes cookies, cake and ice cream. Puppies too.

66579330R00059

Made in the USA
Lexington, KY
18 August 2017